Be a Close-Up Nature Detective

Solving the Tiniest Mysteries
of the Natural World

Text and Artwork by
Peggy Kochanoff

NIMBUS
PUBLISHING
NIMBUS.CA

Copyright © 2024, Peggy Kochanoff

All rights reserved. No part of this book may be reproduced, stored in a retrieval system or transmitted in any form or by any means without the prior written permission from the publisher, or, in the case of photocopying or other reprographic copying, permission from Access Copyright, 1 Yonge Street, Suite 1900, Toronto, Ontario M5E 1E5.

Nimbus Publishing Limited
3660 Strawberry Hill Street, Halifax, NS, B3K 5A9
(902) 455-4286 nimbus.ca

Printed and bound in Canada

NB1766

Editor: Claire Bennet
Design: Jenn Embree

Nimbus Publishing is based in Kjipuktuk, Mi'kma'ki, the traditional territory of the Mi'kmaq People.

Library and Archives Canada Cataloguing in Publication

Title: Be a close-up nature detective : solving the tiniest mysteries of the natural world / text and artwork by Peggy Kochanoff.
Names: Kochanoff, Peggy, 1943- author, illustrator.
Description: Includes bibliographical references.
Identifiers: Canadiana (print) 2024040193X | Canadiana (ebook) 20240401948 | ISBN 9781774713235 (softcover) | ISBN 9781774713242 (EPUB)
Subjects: LCSH: Nature—Juvenile literature. | LCSH: Natural history—Juvenile literature. | LCSH: Ecology—Juvenile literature. | LCGFT: Instructional and educational works.
Classification: LCC QH48 .K63 2024 | DDC j508—dc23

Nimbus Publishing acknowledges the financial support for its publishing activities from the Government of Canada, the Canada Council for the Arts, and from the Province of Nova Scotia. We are pleased to work in partnership with the Province of Nova Scotia to develop and promote our creative industries for the benefit of all Nova Scotians.

Dedicated to my dear sister Kathy Stephen (1945–2022). Miss her lots.

Thanks to my wonderful family (Stan, Tom, Jim, Avai, and Jaya).

Also thanks to Nimbus Publishing for all their help and encouragement and for making the process fun.

Introduction

As we look around in nature, we often miss seeing some amazing things. Not because they are hidden, but because they are very small.

Nature is filled with beautiful, fascinating animals and plants. We tend to think larger ones are more important, but tiny things also have important roles in the environment around us. A tiny seed can become a plant that feeds us and supplies oxygen for us to breathe. A small bee flies around collecting pollen and nectar and in doing so, pollinates the flowers it visits. Without the bees, the majority of our valuable fruits and vegetables wouldn't grow.

Picture yourself the size of a beetle walking through grass the size of trees. Imagine what you can see!

In this book, we'll concentrate on three habitats: a tree, a beach, and a log. When you see the magnifying glass symbol   that means it is time to look closely. Look up definitions to words in **bold** in the glossary at the back of the book (on page 53).

Now, grab your magnifying glass and let's explore the smallest things in nature. Have fun!

What can we find when we look closely at a tree? Let's find out.

Tree Flowers

Do trees have flowers? Hmmm… Let's look closely and find out.

Yes! Trees need to produce pollen and seeds like the plants in your garden. Because plants and trees remain in one place, they need **pollen** to blow through the air and settle in other areas. This helps new plants and trees to grow (and also makes people sneeze)!

Some tree flowers are very small and go unnoticed. Others are showy and attractive.

There are many types of tree flowers, but they are usually divided into "male" and "female" flowers. The male flowers release pollen, while female flowers receive it. Some trees, called **dioecious** trees, have only male or female flowers. Trees with male flowers rely on receiving the pollen from female flowers in order to pollinate. White ash trees, poplar trees, and red maple trees are all dioecious. Red maple flowers bloom before the leaves come out. With red flowers, red twigs, and red buds, they look lovely!

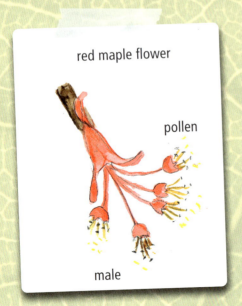

red maple flower
pollen
male

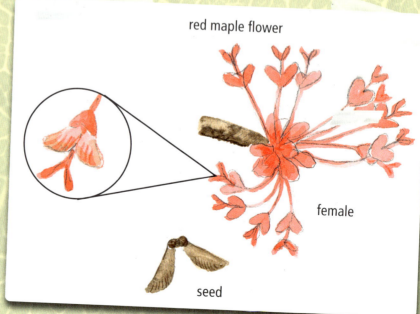

red maple flower
female
seed

Other trees have both male and female flowers. These are called **monoecious** trees. Oak trees, birch trees, and hornbeam trees are all monoecious. Sugar maples are amazing because they can be monoecious or dioecious.

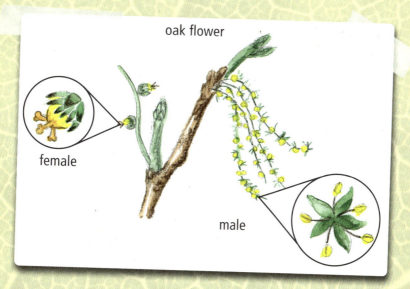

Most of the time, flowers are either male or female—whether they are found on the same tree or different trees. But some flowers known as "perfect flowers" have male *and* female parts on the same bloom. These are found on apple trees, elm trees, and hazelnut trees. These flowers can pollinate themselves!

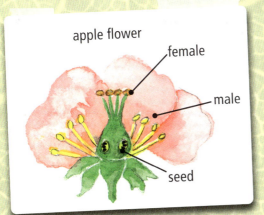

Mystery solved!

9

Tent Caterpillars

What is that icky web in the tree? Hmmm...Let's look closely and find out.

Tent caterpillars hatch from eggs in spring and spin webs in the fork of trees. These shiny webs are known as their "tents." Look at the wiggling caterpillars inside. The tiny dots are poop!

Tent caterpillars shed their skin four to five times as they grow. When they are two inches long, they leave the nest. They spin a cocoon around themselves and hatch two weeks later as moths.

Adult tent caterpillar moths mate, then lay eggs in a web. The outer surface of this web is waterproof so it can survive the winter. Eggs hatch in spring, **larvae** emerge, and the cycle begins again.

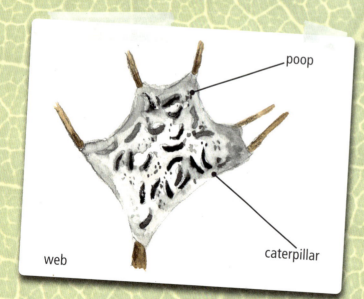

web — poop — caterpillar

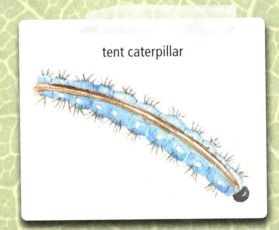

tent caterpillar

egg case

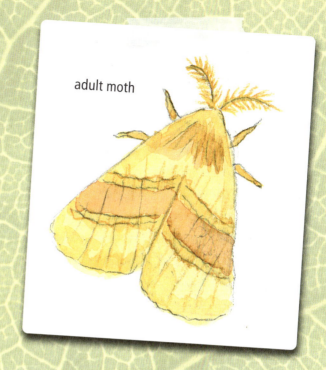

adult moth

Tent caterpillars feed on leaves outside of the tent, but return inside for protection against ants, spiders, birds, and stormy weather. When they go out, they descend to the ground on silk strands and leave a trail of silk to find their way back home.

If there are too many caterpillars, they can defoliate the tree, meaning they can eat all of the leaves on the tree. But the tree usually recovers once the caterpillars become moths.

Mystery solved!

Broken Branches

Who broke these branches? Hmmm… Let's look closely and find out.

Next time you go for a walk in the forest, look carefully at the branches hanging down from trees. If they have ragged edges, they were probably eaten by a deer. We humans have sharp teeth called incisors on the top and bottom of our jaws to help us bite into food. Deer, on the other hand, only have lower incisors, so when they decide to eat a twig, they wrap their tongue around it and rip it off the tree. As a result, the cut looks ragged.

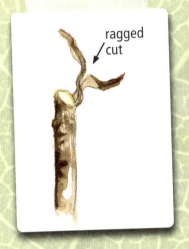

ragged cut

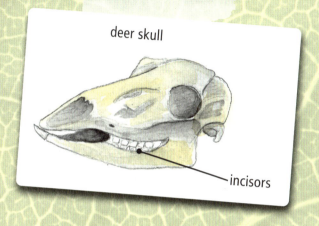

deer skull

incisors

You might find some nibbled twigs with clean edges on the ground. Snowshoe hares have sharp upper and lower teeth that cut twigs at 45-degree angles. So when a snowshoe hare decides to have a snack, the edges of the twig are left with a clean cut.

sharp cut

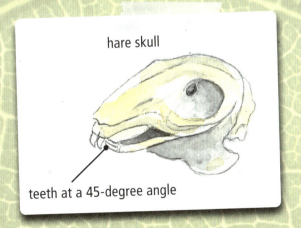

hare skull

teeth at a 45-degree angle

Mystery solved!

Porcupines

> What are those strange marks on the tree trunk? Hmmm... Let's look closely and find out.

Look carefully at the upper part of a tree and you might find places that have been chewed by porcupines. They chew off bark from tree trunks, letting the pieces fall to the ground, then eat the live inner **cambium** layer.

Tree trunks grow in layers. The outer bark protects the tree against insects and extreme weather. Underneath the bark there is the phloem layer, which moves the sugar produced during photosynthesis throughout the rest of the tree. The cambium layer is next, and it helps build the other layers in the trunk. Beneath the layer of cambium is xylem, which moves water and nutrients to every part of the tree. It's the thin cambium layer that porcupines find the most delicious.

Porcupines also eat twigs, leaves, and green plants. Like all rodents, their front teeth grow constantly during their life so chewing helps grind the teeth down and keep them sharp. Because porcupines crave salt, they often eat sweaty objects like work gloves and tool handles. Special bacteria in their fifteen feet of intestines enable them to digest the **cellulose** in wood.

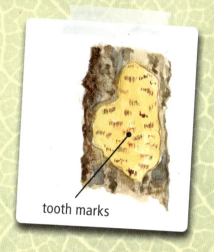

tooth marks

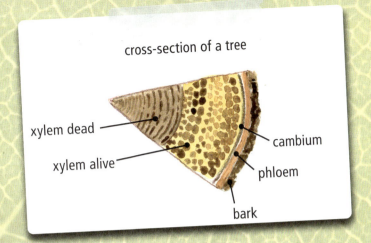

cross-section of a tree

xylem dead, xylem alive, cambium, phloem, bark

Porcupines have poor eyesight and are very slow-moving. For protection, they are covered in prickly spines (up to thirty thousand of them!).

In spite of what you may think, porcupines do not shoot spines at predators, but they release them on contact. On the tip of each spine are tiny backward-facing scales. If they aren't removed from the victim, they will keep moving deeper (sometimes moving one inch a day), and can even cause death. So if you see a porcupine, keep your distance!

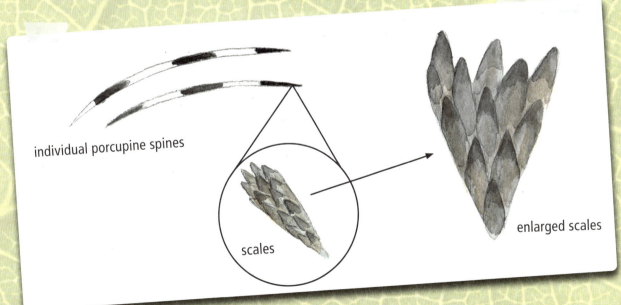

individual porcupine spines

scales

enlarged scales

Mystery solved!

15

Sometimes the bark of a tree looks like it has paint splattered on it. Look closely and you will see it is actually a lichen.

Lichens are made of two organisms living as one, usually fungus and alga. The fungus and alga live together and help each other. This process is called **symbiosis**. The fungus protects the alga, and absorbs water and minerals from the surroundings. Because alga has **chlorophyll**, it can make food for both itself and the fungus.

fruiting bodies that give off spores to grow more lichen

enlarged view

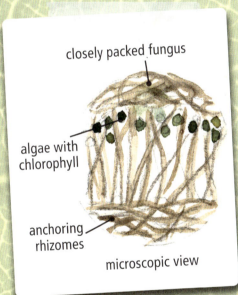

closely packed fungus

algae with chlorophyll

anchoring rhizomes

microscopic view

Lichens are so tough they can survive from the Arctic to the Antarctic, under snow, in hot deserts, on rocks, trees, gravestones, or buildings. They don't need soil to live. Instead, they actually create soil. When lichens are on a rock, they contract when they are dry, and secrete acid. Both of these actions cause tiny rock pieces to crumble and form soil over a long time period.

Mystery solved!

Yellow-Bellied Sapsuckers

Why are there small holes in this tree? Hmmm...Let's look closely and find out.

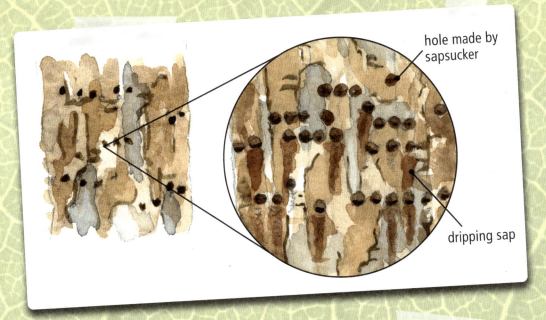

hole made by sapsucker

dripping sap

Yellow-bellied sapsuckers, like the name suggests, like to eat sap from trees. To release the sap, they make lines of small holes on tree trunks. Like all woodpeckers, they bang out these holes with their strong beaks.

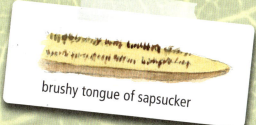

brushy tongue of sapsucker

These birds like to eat the sap from the xylem and phloem layers, which drips from the holes. They lap up the sap with their brushy tongues and eat insects that get stuck in the sap. Half of their diet is from the sap, while the other half is from insects, berries, and fruit. In the spring, hummingbirds feed on this sap after their long migration north.

Sapsuckers only drill holes in trees that have flowing sap. Some of their favourites are maple, aspen, birch, elm, and beech trees. The holes don't necessarily kill trees, but lots of holes around a tree could girdle a section (cause damage all the way around the trunk) and it could die. Holes are also openings for insects and diseases. Some people try to discourage the holes by wrapping tree trunks with burlap or by painting them with a sticky product, but this can be very messy.

Mystery solved!

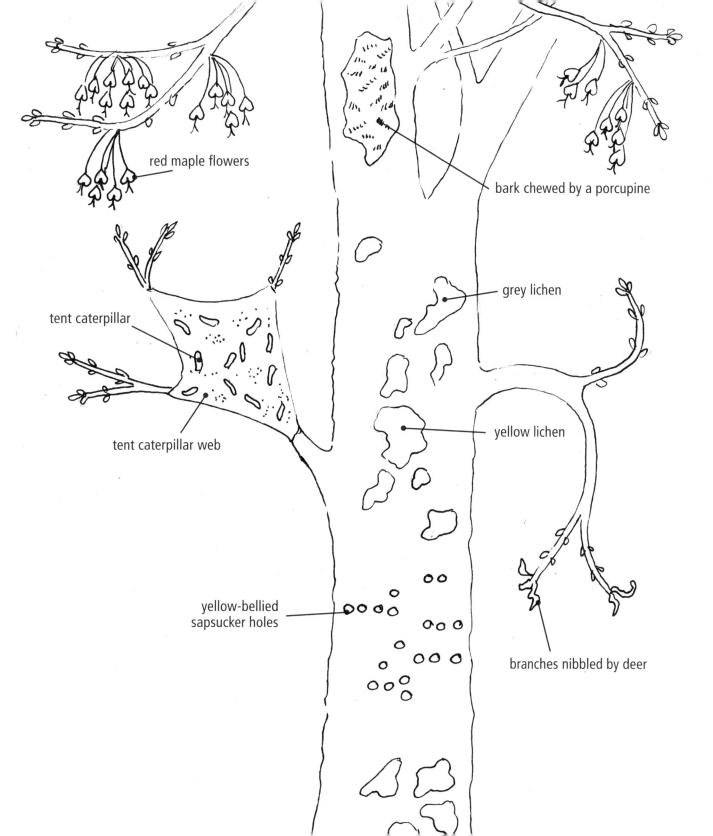

What can we find when we look closely at the beach? Let's find out.

Beach Sand

Is all sand made the same? Hmmm... Let's look closely and find out.

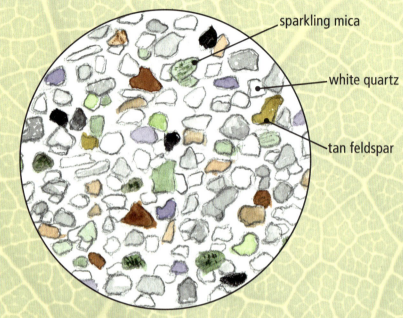

mid-Atlantic and northeast sand

When you walk along a beach, the main thing you will notice is the sand. Sand is formed when rocks and **minerals** are weathered by wind, rain, freezing, and thawing. It might seem like all sand is the same, but look closely and you'll see the small differences.

Sand in the mid-Atlantic and northeastern part of North America is mainly made up of the minerals white quartz, tan feldspar, and sparkling mica. Quartz is the most common component because it doesn't decompose easily or dissolve in water—and there's a lot of water at the beach! You may also find some green hornblende, purple garnet, and a little magnetite. If you run a magnet over some sand, the magnetite will stick to it!

The soil on Prince Edward Island contains lots of iron, so when it rains or traps a lot of moisture, the soil rusts (**oxidizes**) and turns red. The beaches often contain some amount of soil and iron, so the sand is red too!

In Florida and some tropical islands, sand is made of a lot of pulverized shells, coral, and marine animal skeletons, which makes it very white and soft.

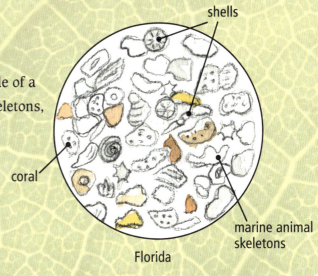
Florida

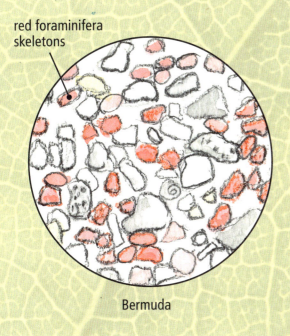
Bermuda

There is a pink tinge to the sand in Bermuda. Tiny **invertebrates** living in the area, called red foraminifera, have small red spherical skeletons. When these break up, the pieces colour the sand pink.

On beaches in Hawaii, a lot of eroded black volcanic rock can be found among the quartz grains of sand.

On your next vacation be sure to bring your magnifying glass to look at the beach sand.

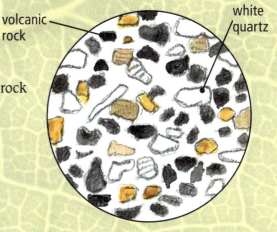
Hawaii

Mystery solved!

Beach Fleas

What are those tiny jumping critters? Hmmm… Let's look closely and find out.

Debris—like logs, sticks, grass, and seaweed—often collects along the beach, providing a nice home for small critters called beach fleas. When the debris is disturbed, the beach fleas jump away from it. They can jump over a metre high!

Despite the name, they are NOT actually fleas—or even insects at all. Beach fleas are marine **crustaceans** similar to crabs, lobsters, and crayfish. Beach fleas look like pale, flat, sandy-coloured shrimp and are less than two centimetres long. They spend most of their time scavenging, feeding on decaying animals and plants. Overall, these jumping creatures are completely harmless.

Mystery solved!

Rockweed

What is that slimy brown plant growing over the rocks? Hmmm…Let's look closely and find out.

Those leathery brown fronds belong to a type of seaweed called rockweed. Like the name suggests, rockweed usually covers rocks, but often washes ashore after storms.

Along each frond of rockweed, you'll find small, round balloons known as a floatation bladders. These are filled with air and help keep the fronds afloat. Try popping one open with your fingers!

The bumpy sacs at the end of each frond contain male and female cells. The cells reproduce in winter and early spring to help grow and spread the rockweed. You can tell which are male and which are female by their colour. When opened, male sacs are orange and female sacs are olive.

Large mats of rockweed make a great shelter for many sea animals, like periwinkles, limpets, hydroids, tube worms, and sea anemones.

Lots of people use this seaweed as a fertilizer or mulch in their garden. It can also be turned into vitamin-rich and nutritious pet food and livestock feed, or even used in paint and makeup!

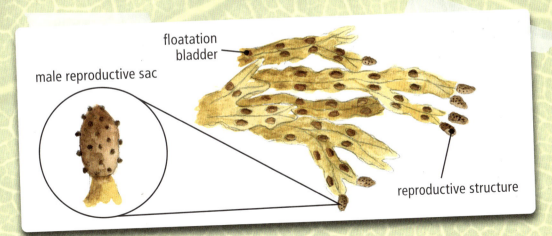

male reproductive sac — floatation bladder — reproductive structure

Mystery solved!

27

Moon Snails

Why is the sand stuck together in a circle? Hmmm... Let's look closely and find out.

moon snail
foot

As you walk along the water's edge, look in the shallows for sand collars. These half-circle sand formations are created by moon snails laying eggs in the sand.

Female moon snails each have one huge, gushy foot that they use to cover their body with sand. They stick this sand to their body with mucus. They then lay eggs and cover themselves with another sand layer so the eggs are sandwiched against their body. Sometimes they lay thousands of eggs at one time!

After 10–14 hours, the snail leaves the rubbery circle they made of sand, mucus, and eggs. To exit, they create an opening, so now the circle looks like a collar. If you find a wet sand collar, hold it up to the sun. The spots you see are actual tiny little eggs! After a few weeks, the eggs hatch and the collar disintegrates. Be gentle with the collars you find, and return them to the water.

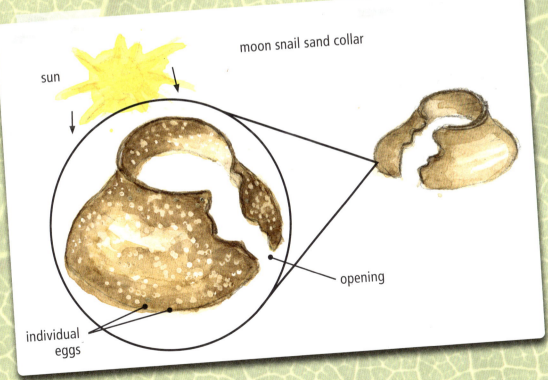
sun
moon snail sand collar
opening
individual eggs

Mystery solved!

29

Sea Sponges

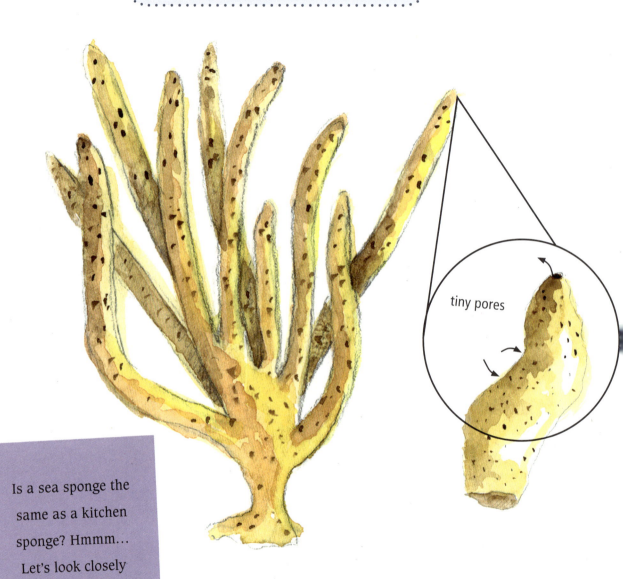

tiny pores

Is a sea sponge the same as a kitchen sponge? Hmmm... Let's look closely and find out.

After a big storm, you might find pieces of finger sponge washed up on the beach. This sponge looks like a thin hand with many long fingers.

Though it looks a bit like seaweed underwater, sponges are not plants. They are the most primitive multi-celled animal. They have no mouth, stomach, or other internal organs, so individual cells perform specific tasks to keep the sponge alive. Sea water enters the sponge through tiny pores, just like water might enter a kitchen sponge at home. Hair-like **flagella** push the water through the sponge's central canal, where oxygen and **organic** particles, such as plankton, are filtered from the water to feed the sponge. Tough needle-shaped fibres called spicules make the sponge firm. The water leaves through a larger hole on top.

So while a sea sponge acts just like a synthetic sponge you might find in your kitchen or bathroom, it's actually a living animal!

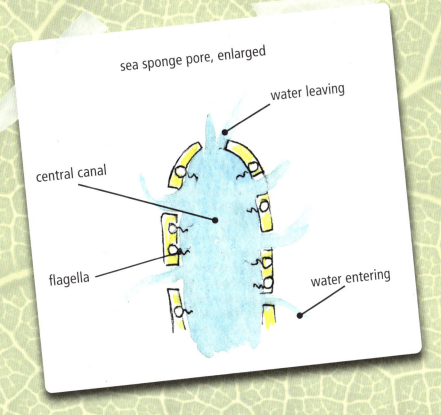

Mystery solved!

Look in the shallows for living starfish (also called sea stars). The red spot on top, called a sieve plate, is where sea water is pumped in and out of the starfish. Along each of the starfish's arms are tube feet. At the end of the tube feet are suckers, 🔍 which, together with the arm muscles, are extremely strong. As sea water moves through the starfish, its tube feet lengthen and contract. With the pulsing sea water and the contracting tube feet, the starfish uses its suckers to stick to the ground and walk in whatever direction it chooses. They move an average of one metre per minute.

Starfish are so strong they can actually pry open a clam. After prying it open, they push their stomach into the clam, releasing enzymes that digest the clam. Then the starfish pulls their stomach back inside their body.

Starfish also have eyes! Look for a small red eye at the tip of each arm. 🔍 It can only detect lightness and darkness.

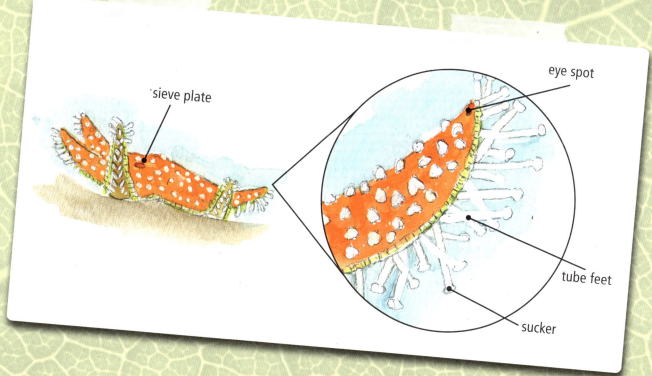

Mystery solved!

33

What can we find when we look closely at a log? Let's find out.

Fern Spores

How do plants reproduce without seeds? Hmmm… Let's look closely and find out.

Ferns are one of the oldest plants on the planet.

They don't produce seeds, and instead reproduce with tiny **spores**. Spores are single cells, unlike seeds, which are made up of multiple different cells and parts. Spores are very hardy, meaning they can survive in even the darkest and harshest conditions. They are also very, very small.

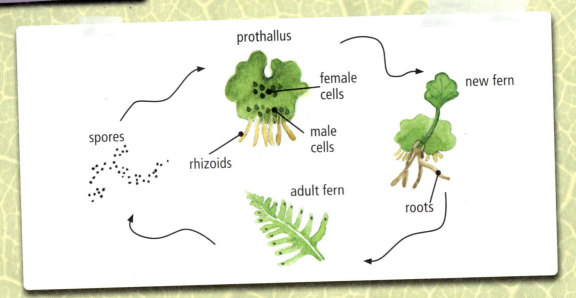

When the air is dry, the fern spores scatter. When a spore lands on the ground, it grows into tiny heart-shaped plants called a **prothallus**. These plants eventually grow into new ferns. **Rhizoids** (horizontal stems) anchor the prothallus. Roots grow out of the bottom and take up water. Once the new fern develops, the prothallus dries up. New ferns can also sprout from underground stems or leaf tips.

The ferns that died millions of years ago formed the coal and oil we use today!

Different types of ferns are identified by their leaves, habitat, and the shape and placement of their spores. Because most spore cases grow on the underside of the fronds, or leaves, some gardeners mistakenly think they are signs of disease or insects.

Mystery solved!

Fungi

> How do fungi get food? Hmmm... Let's look closely and find out.

Fungi (the plural of fungus), such as mushrooms, don't have roots, stems, leaves, flowers, or seeds so they aren't really plants.

Most plants contain a green pigment called chlorophyll that helps them make their own food. But fungi don't have chlorophyll, so they take food from the soil, decaying wood, and vegetable matter around them.

A network of very tiny and thin strands called mycelium grows underground. These mycelium absorb food for the fungus. Mycelium can live for decades, even centuries! When the ground is moist, the mycelium swell and push above the surface. This fleshy plant is the fruiting body (like flowers in our garden) for fungi. It produces spores (instead of seeds) to grow more fungus. These fruiting bodies are the part of the mushroom or other fungi we're most familiar with, and can be shaped like cups, stalks, brackets, or balls.

The most familiar type of fungus is a gill fungus, which has a stalk and cap on top. If you look underneath the cup, you'll find thin, sheet-like gills from which spores fall.

Pore fungi (like this turkey tail fungi) have inner tubes on their underside. Spores are released through the tubes. These fungi usually feel leathery on the outside.

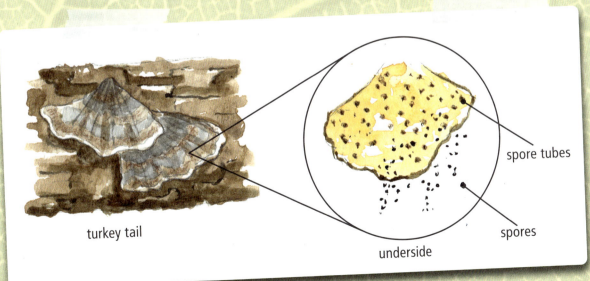

Bird's nest fungi are amazing. They look like tiny bird's nests with eggs inside (these eggs are the fruiting bodies). Rain usually splashes the spores out of the nest.

These irregular, yellow-orange gelatinous fungi are called witch's butter. Imagine a witch eating a bread and butter sandwich, and some butter oozes out—that's what this fungi looks like. The spores are released from the jelly-like lobes.

Witch's butter is actually an edible fungus! Like anything you forage in the woods, be sure to ask an adult before eating it. Most foragers recommend cooking mushrooms instead of eating them raw.

Mystery solved!

Pill Bugs

How does a small grey pill bug help put nutrients into the soil? Hmmm…Let's look closely and find out.

Have you ever tickled a pill bug and watched it curl into a ball? It's funny and cute to see, but to the bug, it's an important defence against predators.

Pill bugs (also called potato bugs or roly-polies) are land animals, but belong to an aquatic family that also includes shrimp, lobster, and crabs. They live in damp, dark places under floorboards, bark, soil, stones, and rotting wood. As scavengers, they eat decaying plant matter like wood and leaves. After they digest this food, they poop it out and the plant matter nourishes the soil.

Mystery solved!

Slugs

How do squishy slugs stay safe from predators? Hmmm... Let's look closely and find out.

These funny little creatures look like snails without shells. Because they don't have shells, they can squeeze into small spaces. But they are also more exposed to sun, wind, and predators, so they often hide in damp places.

When touched, slugs contract so they look like fat worms. On their heads are two eyestalks for vision and smell. Nearby are two smaller stalks for touch and taste. 🔍 These stalks look like antennae. Touch them gently and watch them contract.

Slugs secrete a film of mucus both to help prevent their skin from drying out and to slide along the ground more easily. The mucus also makes it harder for a predator to pick the slug up—and it tastes bad so the predators don't want to eat the slug.

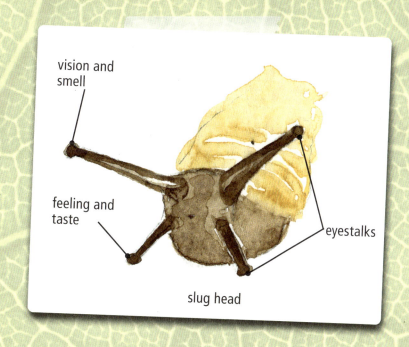

Mystery solved!

45

Moss

How does a blanket of moss grow? Hmmm... Let's look closely and find out.

Among the bark of a decaying log you will probably find lots of fuzzy, green moss. It's found in damp, shady places (not just on the north side of trees as many people think). Moss grows everywhere, from the cold Arctic to humid and warm tropical islands, on trees, rocks, and soil. When moss dies, it decays and becomes soil.

When moss spore cases release spores, the spores **germinate**. Green threads form from the spore and a bud develops. These become male and female plants. During moist weather, the male cells fertilize the female cells, and a new plant begins to grow.

To identify mosses, look at the form of the plant and shape of the capsules.

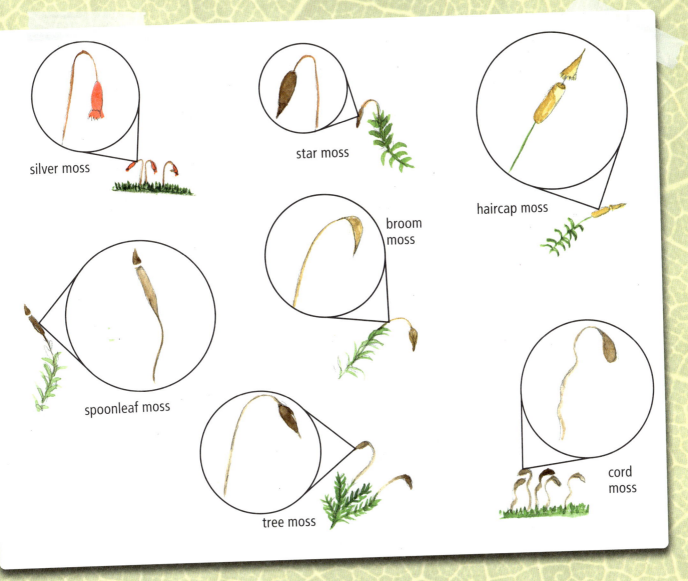

Mystery solved!

Millipedes and Centipedes

How many feet do millipedes and centipedes really have? Hmmm…Let's look closely and find out.

We usually jump when a millipede or centipede creeps by, but you don't need to be afraid of them. Interestingly, neither creature is an insect. They are **arthropods** like crabs, shrimp, and lobsters.

Millipedes have two pairs of legs (four legs total) on each segment of their body. Even though "millipede" means "one thousand feet," they don't actually have that many feet. Most have around three hundred legs, but it can vary anywhere from forty to four hundred legs. Their legs point toward the ground.

Millipedes are slow moving and don't bite. To scare away predators, they curl up and may give off a smelly secretion. They are scavengers, and prefer to eat dead leaves and decaying wood.

millipede

Centipedes have one pair of legs (two legs total) on each segment of their body. But even though "centipede" means "one hundred feet," they usually don't have as many as one hundred legs. Most centipedes have around thirty legs, but some have up to four hundred! Their legs point away from their body.

Unlike millipedes, centipedes are fast and can bite. They bite their prey with the first pair of appendages behind their head, releasing venom from the claw-like jaws to paralyze their prey. They like to eat pests in your house like spiders, bedbugs, cockroaches, silverfish, and ants. Their venom doesn't harm humans unless you are allergic.

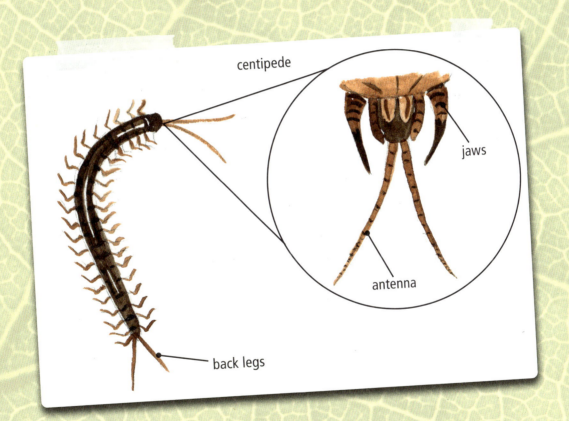

Mystery solved!

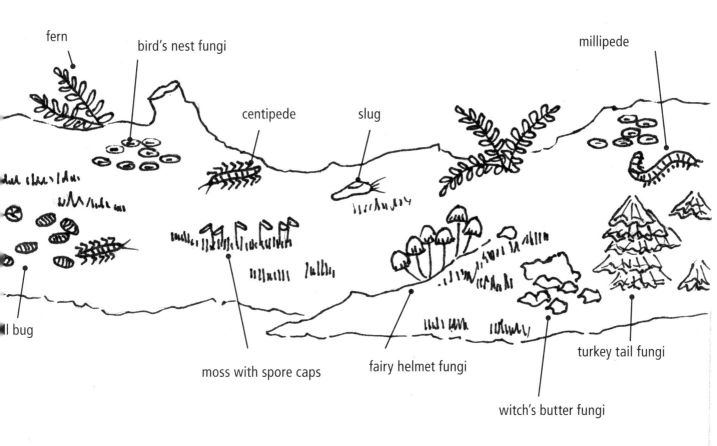

Close-up Nature Adventure

Go on a mini safari with your magnifying glass! Please leave items from nature where you find them. Instead, draw pictures in a journal to keep a record of what you find.

Flowers

Look at different kinds of flowers and try to find the male and female parts. Remember, not every flower will have both.

Tree Trunks

Walk around and look at tree trunks. Some have deep grooves, some are smooth, and others have patches of lichen. What else do you notice?

Insects

Insects are fascinating, whether alive or dead. You might have better luck observing a dead insect since it won't move away. Look for insects that are different sizes and shapes. Look for glistening wings, prickly legs, and different shapes of antennae.

Soil

Look at the soil in different places and see if the grain size and colour is different. What does the texture of soil feel like? How is it different when it is wet or dry?

Leaves

Leaves come in all kinds of sizes and shapes. Look for round ones, pointy ones, tiny ones, and big ones.

Glossary

Arthropods: A large group of invertebrates with segmented bodies, jointed appendages, and an external skeleton (like spiders and crustaceans).

Cambium: The live inner layer on a tree after the bark and phloem. It creates new cells to allow the tree to grow.

Cellulose: The main substance found in plant cells, which helps the plant keep its shape.

Chlorophyll: A green pigment in plants that uses energy from the sun, water, and carbon dioxide to produce oxygen and food.

Crustacean: A large class of mostly aquatic animals with a hard exoskeleton, often with modified appendages and two pairs of antennae. Lobsters, shrimp, crabs, barnacles, and water fleas are all examples of crustaceans.

Dioecious: A type of tree that produces either male or female flowers. White ash, poplar, and red maple trees are all examples of dioecious trees.

Flagella: Microscopic hair-like structures that help a cell move through liquid. These are found on finger sponges and help water move through the inside of the sponge.

Fungi: Organisms that have no roots, stems, leaves, flowers, or seeds, so they are not plants. These include mushrooms, moulds, and yeasts.

Germinate: When a spore or seed starts to grow.

Invertebrate: An animal with a soft body that has no internal skeleton (but it might have a hard outer skeleton that helps protect the body). This includes 90 percent of living animal species, such as sea sponges, insects, and snails.

Larva: A young animal or insect that changes into another form in adulthood. More than one larva is called larvae.

Mineral: A solid substance found in nature that is neither a plant nor an animal. Minerals make up rocks, clays, sand, and other similar materials.

Monoecious: A type of tree that produces both male and female flowers on the same tree. Oak, birch, and hornbeam trees are all examples of monoecious trees.

Organic: A word used to describe items found in nature that come from living things.

Oxidize: When something combines with oxygen. When soil with a high iron content, like the soil on Prince Edward Island, oxidizes, it turns red.

Pollen: A fine powder produced by certain plants that causes the plants to form seeds. Pollen is formed in the male plant structure to help the plant reproduce.

Prothallus: The part of a fern attached to the soil by rhizoids. The prothallus produces male or female cells and helps the fern to grow.

Rhizoids: Horizontal stems that grow beneath certain plants, like ferns.

Spore: A reproductive part that is made up of one single cell. It can grow into a new organism without combining with another reproductive cell.

Symbiosis: Two organisms living together and helping each other.

References

Kochanoff, Peggy. *A Field Guide to Nearby Nature: Fields and Woods of the Midwest and East Coast.* Missoula, Montana: Mountain Press Pub., 1994.

Kochanoff, Peggy. *Beachcombing the Atlantic Coast.* Missoula, Montana: Mountain Press Pub., 1997.

Latimer, Jonathan and Nolting, Karen. *Caterpillars.* Boston: Houghton Mifflin Co., 1980.

Zim, Herbert and Ingle, Lester. *Seashores: A Guide to Animals and Plants along the Beaches.* New York: Simon and Schuster, 1955.

Collect all the books in the Be a Nature Detective series!

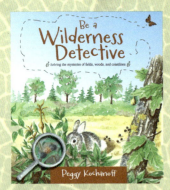

978-1-77108-012-5

Shortlisted 2015 Silver Birch Express Award

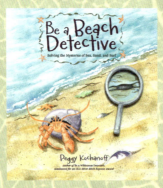

978-1-77108-267-9

Shortlisted 2017 Hackmatack Award

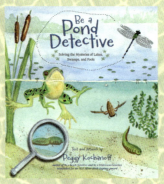

978-1-77108-394-2

Shortlisted 2017 Silver Birch Express Award

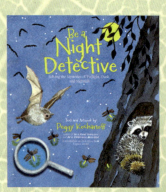

978-1-77108-464-2

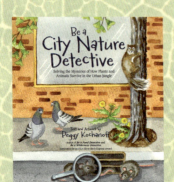

978-1-77108-572-4

2019 TD Summer Reading Club Selection

978-1-77108-796-4

Shortlisted 2021–22 Hackmatack Award

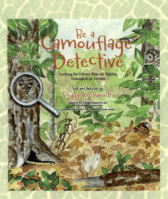

978-1-77471-000-5

Available at bookstores everywhere and at nimbus.ca